A CLAIRE SHARES BOOK

ISABELLE
THE IBD WARRIOR

Kendra & Claire MOORE

illustrated by Allie-Marie Piggott

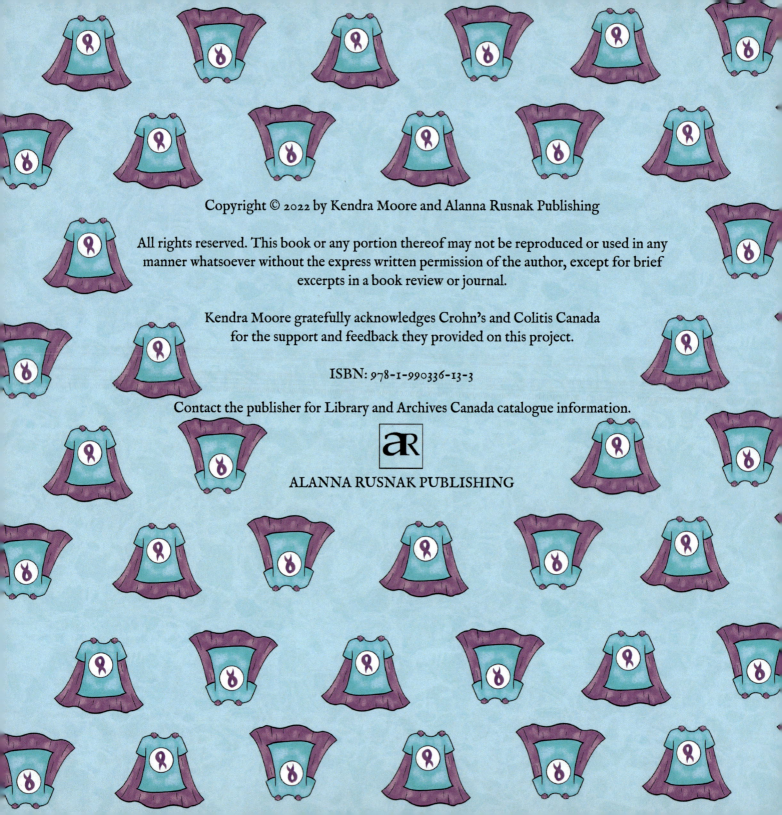

Copyright © 2022 by Kendra Moore and Alanna Rusnak Publishing

All rights reserved. This book or any portion thereof may not be reproduced or used in any manner whatsoever without the express written permission of the author, except for brief excerpts in a book review or journal.

Kendra Moore gratefully acknowledges Crohn's and Colitis Canada for the support and feedback they provided on this project.

ISBN: 978-1-990336-13-3

Contact the publisher for Library and Archives Canada catalogue information.

ALANNA RUSNAK PUBLISHING

Hi! My name is Isabelle and I am 9 years old.

This is my bear called Clairebear. She helps me when I am scared or worried.

I have something called IBD - that stands for Inflammatory Bowel Disease. Anyone who has this disease is an IBD Warrior. Do you know why?

Because anyone who is an IBD Warrior is super strong! Are you super strong?

Inflammatory Bowel Disease

Inflammatory Bowel Disease - or IBD - is a chronic disease that makes your digestive tract get inflamed.

That's a lot of big words, huh?

Let me explain it for you.

Your digestive tract is all the parts of your body that food travels through.

It starts in your mouth and goes down a tube into your stomach. Your stomach breaks it down and then pushes it through your small and large intestine. Your small intestine soaks up all the nutrients and vitamins and your large intestine soaks up water and salt.

Once that's done, you poop out the stuff your body doesn't need.

This is a picture of your digestive tract:

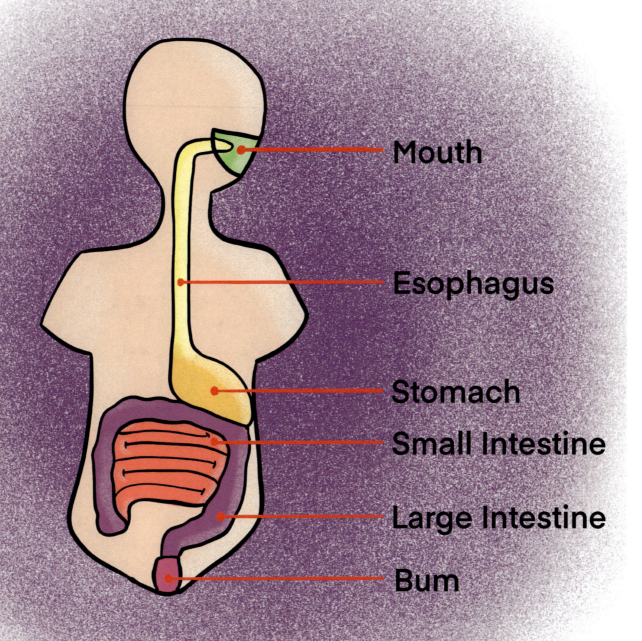

The word "chronic" means that it is an illness you will have for your whole life. With IBD, you will have episodes where you will feel good and episodes where you may feel sick. There is no cure yet, but those smart scientists are getting closer all the time! That may not sound so good to you right now, especially if you are feeling as sick as I did, but it does get better.

I used to feel sick and yucky but now I feel great, thanks to medicine!

Right now, I don't feel any different than any of my family or friends.

Now, let's talk about what that word "Inflammation" or "inflamed" means.

These words mean that whatever is inflamed looks red and angry. Do you ever get so mad that your face turns red? This is kind of what your insides are doing.

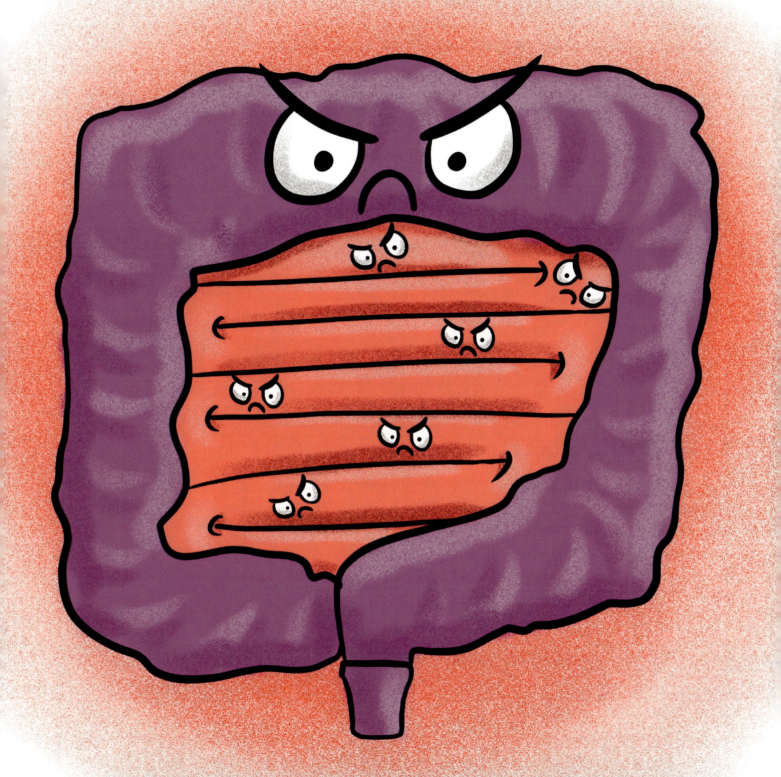

When your insides are red and angry, it can cause you to feel sick or have pain around your tummy, and it might make you have to go to the bathroom A LOT.

Having diarrhea can make it hard to do things and it doesn't feel very nice. It can also make you feel tired and sometimes you might not have enough energy to want to play or do many activities.

We don't always know what made them so angry but that's okay; the important thing is, we can learn how to help make you feel better.

It all sounds pretty scary, right?

I was scared too and really glad I had Clairebear to hold, but don't worry, there is medicine that can help!

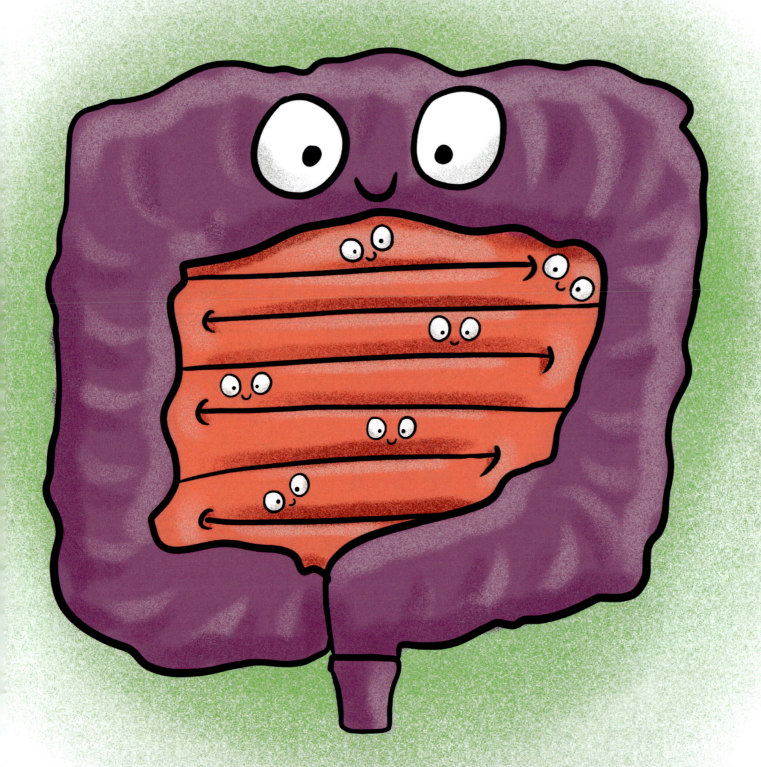

Medicine can turn those red, angry faces
into happy, smiley faces!

There are two kinds of IBD.

One is called Crohn's Disease, the other is called Ulcerative Colitis.

Crohn's Disease causes inflammation - remember that word? Think red, angry faces that show up anywhere from your mouth to your bum.

Ulcerative Colitis can cause inflammation in your large intestine only. Look at the picture to see. Purple is where Crohn's might happen, green shows Ulcerative Colitis.

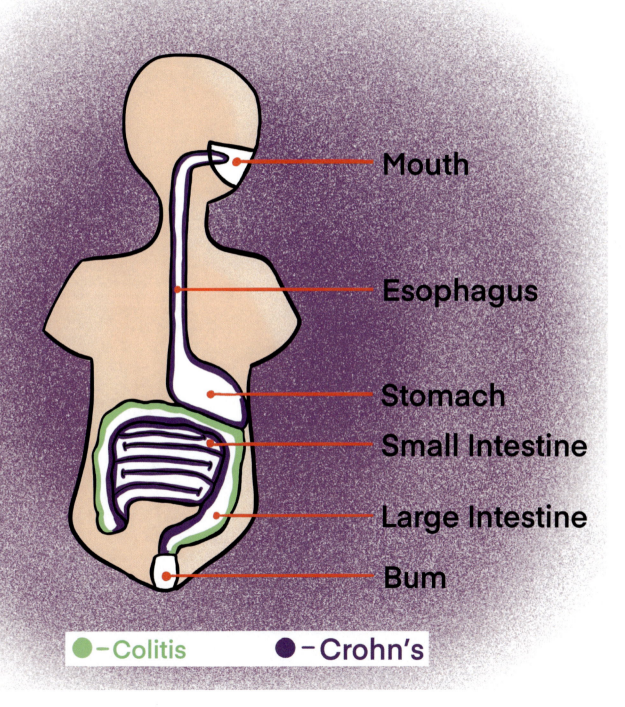

Sometimes, if your insides stay red and angry for too long, it might cause ulcers.

Ulcers are sores inside your body that can bleed, so you might see blood in your poop if that happens.

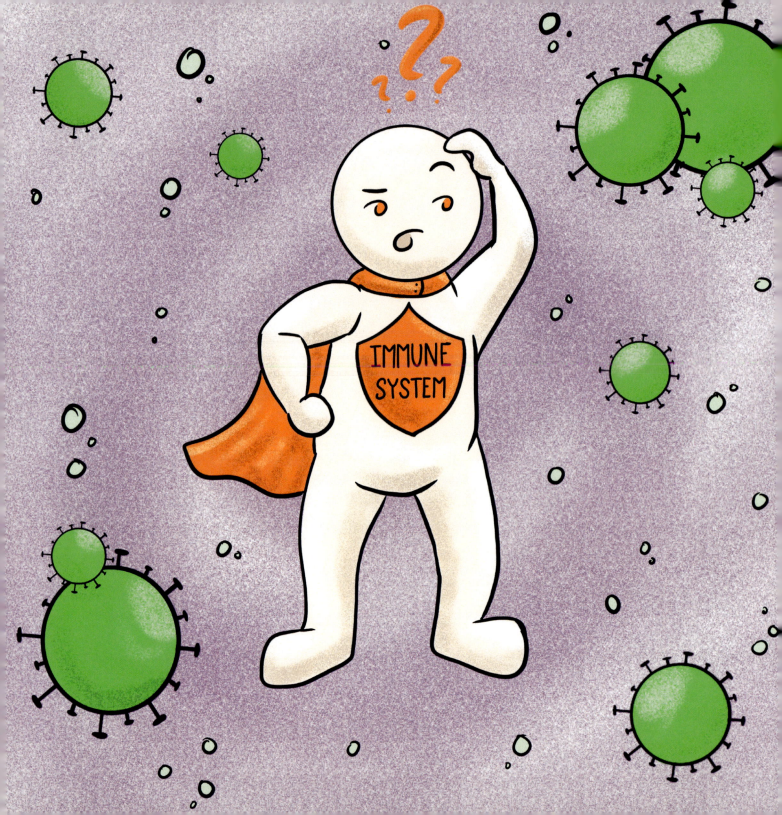

IBD is something called an autoimmune disease. Here come the big words again!

Having an autoimmune disease kind of means that your immune system is confused. Do you know what your immune system is?

Everybody gets sick sometimes, but it's your immune system that helps you get better. Think of your immune system as your own little fighter army.

Pretend you have a cold. That cold germ in your body is the enemy. Your immune system is going to send off the warning bells that there is an invader and they need to be stopped. Your fighter army marches out to surround that cold germ and defeat it.

That is the job of your immune system.

Once your fighter army has won, that cold germ is gone and you are better.

Your immune system is the winner!

Our bodies are full of germs, but did you know that not all germs are bad? There are good germs too. We need good germs in our bodies to help keep us healthy.

GOOD GERM

BAD GERM

But with an autoimmune disease, your immune system forgets what germs are good and what germs are bad. Because it is confused, it is sending out your fighter army to not only attack the bad things in your body, but it is telling them to attack the good things too.

You see, when your immune system tries to fight the good things in your body, it can make you sick.

Imagine...the thing that is supposed to keep you healthy, is making you sick.

Your body has too many fighters. So, to help with this, there is a special kind of medicine that keeps some fighters working to fight off the bad things, but it puts some fighters to sleep so they don't attack the good things.

I know when my doctor first told me I had IBD I was scared. The words were so big and I didn't understand what was happening.

Every single feeling you are feeling right now is completely normal.

It's okay to feel scared, or angry, or confused, or anything else you feel.

I learned that it's SO important for me to ask questions and to talk to a grown up about all my feelings.

It always makes me feel a lot better.

I want to tell you that having IBD does not mean you will feel sick forever. You can feel good even if you have IBD. Medicine is pretty amazing, so trust your doctors and grown ups.

Everyone's experience is different and there are some more tests that you may have to do, but I believe in you and I know that you can do hard things, just like I can.

You are now an IBD Warrior just like me!

Go Warriors!!

Questions I have:

My worries:

My thoughts:

My feelings:

Claire is the IBD Warrior upon whom Isabelle is based, and Kendra is the lucky one who gets to be her mother. Together, Kendra and Claire are writing books inspired by Claire's personal experience through her own journey with IBD since her 2020 diagnosis. Claire has a vision to help other kids in similar situations and it is their hope that these books can make your child feel a little more comfortable with becoming an IBD Warrior.

Claire is an active volunteer with Crohn's and Colitis Canada with the Gutsy Walk being her largest donation event. She has been honoured to have been the Local Honourary Chair for her community as well as the National Honourary Chair of this yearly event. Gutsy Walk is held in local communities across Canada to help raise awareness and funds for Crohn's and Colitis Canada in hopes of finding a cure for IBD someday soon.

Claire lives with her mom, Kendra, her dad, Brent, her big sister, Avery and her puppy Nessa in the village of Ayton Ontario. Claire loves to go horseback riding, dance and play with her friends and sister.

Allie-Marie Piggott is an aspiring artist who grew up in the Bridgeport Kitchener area, but currently lives in London, Ontario. Originally self-taught, she went on to study Design Foundations at Conestoga College and then Illustration and Concept Art at Algonquin College in Ottawa. She works with a multitude of different media allowing herself to be very versatile, and has had the true pleasure of working with a variety of clients for a number of different commissions. Allie-Marie is a passionate artist who loves creating artwork either for herself or others, and she cannot wait for what comes next.

Manufactured by Amazon.ca
Bolton, ON